The TIME *trekkers* visit the DINOSAURS

KATE NEEDHAM

COPPER BEECH

BROOKFIELD, CONNECTICUT

© Aladdin Books Ltd 1995

Designed and produced by
Aladdin Books Ltd
28 Percy Street
London W1P 0LD

First published in 1995 in the
United States by
Copper Beech Books, an imprint of
The Millbrook Press
2 Old New Milford Road
Brookfield, Connecticut 06804

Editor
Jim Pipe
Designed by
David West Children's Books
Designer
Simon Morse
Illustrated by
Sheena Vickers
Additional illustrations by
David Burroughs

Printed in Belgium

Library of Congress Cataloging-in-
Publication

Needham, Kate.
The dinosaurs / by Kate Needham :
illustrated by Sheena Vickers and
Dave Burroughs.
p. cm. - (The time trekkers visit the--)
Includes index.
Summary: Presents information on the
ancient world of the dinosaurs
including a chapter on digging for
fossils and discussion of the
compsognathus, stegasaurus,
pterosaurs, and others.
ISBN 1-56294-942-X (lib. bdg.)
1-56294-196-8 (pbk.)
1. Dinosaurs--Juvenile literature. [1.
Dinosaurs.] I. Vickers, Sheena. ill.
II. Burroughs, Dave. 1952- ill. III.
Title. IV. Series.
QE862.D5N44 1995   95-14023
567.9 1--dc20   CIP
                          AC

INTRODUCTION
The Time trekkers

The Time trekkers are Lucy, Jools, Eddie, and Sam. Using the time machine invented by Lucy's eccentric grandfather, they travel through time and space on amazing voyages of discovery. Their gizmos are always ready to answer any questions!

But before we follow their journey back to the world of the dinosaurs, let's meet the four adventurers...

Lucy – As the oldest of the four, Lucy can be a bit bossy. But when the going gets tough, the others rely on her to save the day.

Jools is always in a rush, but when he does stop, he usually gets caught up in the local wildlife. Look out for his pet frog, Kevin.

Eddie – With his knowledge of history, it's Eddie's job to set the controls on the time machine. But he does have a tendency to drift off into a dreamworld of his own!

Sam – When the time machine starts acting up, call Sam, the Time trekkers' whiz kid. She's great with gizmos and all kinds of gadgets, but sometimes gets so wrapped up in her portable stereo, she doesn't notice the danger around her!

The Gizmo

To use this book, simply read the Time trekkers' question bubbles, then look to the gizmo for the answer! There are three subject buttons:

- 🔍 *Science (Orange)*
- ⊕ *Places and People (Purple)*
- 🕐 *History and Arts (Red)*

And two extra special functions:

- ☠ *X ray (Yellow)*
- **T** *Translator (Blue)*

TRICERATOPS
(Tri-ser-ah-tops) "THREE-HORNED FACE"

- **Weight:** Up to 5.5 tons • **Length:** 29 feet
- **Age:** 70 million years • **Food:** Plants
- **Features:** Frills to protect its neck; horns for charging rivals; a parrotlike beak.

Subject logo

Translator panel tells you how to pronounce dinosaur names and what these names mean.

Gizmo's answer

Control panels

One sunny day, the Time trekkers were at a fossil dig. A team of experts was busy digging up a huge dinosaur called Triceratops. Sam and Eddie found a bone which was taller than both of them, and that was just part of a leg!

"I wouldn't like to meet one of these while it was around," said Sam. "Well," boasted Eddie, "they don't scare me." But before he knew it, Sam was racing home to the time machine. "Come on everyone," she shouted, "let's see how tough Eddie really is!"

What was this dinosaur called?

It must have been enormous!

TRICERATOPS
(Tri-ser-ah-tops) "THREE-HORNED FACE"

Skeleton

Skeleton with muscles

- **Weight:** Up to 5.5 tons • **Length:** 30 feet
- **Age:** 65 million years • **Food:** Plants
- **Features:** Frills to protect its neck; horns for charging rivals; a parrotlike beak.

4

After a bumpy ride back through 150 million years – Wham! – they reached the Jurassic period. Jools stepped out into a hot, steamy forest. There were no people, no cars, and the air was full of strange sounds and smells. In the distance, something rumbled. Jools looked around nervously, expecting a huge dinosaur to pounce at any moment, but the only creatures he could see were barely knee-high.

Then Sam spotted a giant footprint. She sat down to get a better view, and called over to Lucy. But when Lucy turned around, Sam had vanished!

They look more like chickens!

What are those little dinosaurs?

COMPSOGNATHUS
(Komp-sog-nath-us) "ELEGANT JAW"

- Length: 27.5 inches
- Weight: 7 pounds
- Age: 150 million years (twice as old as Triceratops).
- Food: Insects and lizards (right and below).
- Features: Small, fast, with bones like a bird; its skeleton is similar to a modern crow.

6

How long *is* this neck?

The others fought their way through the thick carpet of ferns to find Sam. But the rock that she had sat on was actually the head of a Diplodocus. As it lifted its head, Sam tumbled down its long neck onto its back!

Meanwhile, Jools couldn't believe his eyes. A whole herd of these giant creatures was calmly grazing on the trees. They seemed very peaceful, but when one of them took a step, the ground shook with a great rumble. Suddenly, spotting a different dinosaur in the distance, Jools ran across for a closer look.

DIPLODOCUS
(Dip-lod-oh-kus) "DOUBLE BEAM"

- **Length:** 90 feet – and 35 feet is its neck!
- **Weight:** Up to 25 tons – more than the combined weight of four elephants.
- **Age:** 150 million years.
- **Features:** It uses its whiplash tail and size against predators (animals that hunt). It is also protected by belonging to a herd.

I wonder if its feet ache?

How does it digest its food?

STOMACH STONES

Diplodocus uses its small teeth to scrape leaves from a branch. Since these teeth are weak, food is swallowed whole and broken down in its stomach. Tough stomach muscles squeeze and pound the food to break it down.

Some dinosaurs swallow stones (about 4 inches across) to help their stomachs break down the food in the same way as a bird's gizzard. These stones (*right*) become incredibly smooth from all the grinding.

HIGH HEELS!

Diplodocus   *Elephant*

Be careful where you stand Jools, you know how big elephant droppings are!

Diplodocus has wide, round feet like an elephant's, with pads at the back. These help to spread its body weight, and the pads act like the heels on our shoes, making it easier to walk. The sharp thumb claw on each foot may be used for fighting.

Jools scrambled straight up onto the back of a Stegosaurus to take a closer look at its jagged plates. Eddie thought this was far too risky, and decided to double-check what it was eating first. Sam was more worried about being trampled on, while Lucy dodged its spiked tail.

In all the excitement, no one noticed a rapidly approaching shadow. There was a loud flapping noise, a flashing shape, and whooosh... Jools was swept into the air by a gigantic bird!

What are the spikes for?

STEGOSAURUS

(Steg-ah-saw-rus) "ROOF LIZARD"

- Length: 25 feet
- Weight: 2 tons
- Age: 150 million years
- Food: Plants
- Features: Be careful Lucy!

The stegosaurus uses its large, spiked tail to defend itself against oncoming meat-eaters.

It either takes a swipe using the weight of the tail, or backs into attackers with its spikes.

How much does it weigh?

The giant bird was actually a hungry pterosaur which grabbed Jools by the hood of his sweatshirt. As it took off toward the forest, Jools struggled to free himself from its grasp. By a stroke of luck, he slipped out of his jacket, bounced through the trees, and landed on a soft bed of ferns right next to the time machine!

Sam was already inside, and the others were on their way. As he climbed in, Jools tripped and fell against the controls. To his horror, the doors closed, and in an instant, they were sent hurtling through time!

Have those dinosaurs got feathers?

Look out Jools, it's got teeth!

PTEROSAURS

(Tair-o-soars) "WINGED REPTILES"

Those sharp teeth belong to a pterosaur. These aren't dinosaurs, although they are closely related. They resemble birds, but they were actually reptiles. Two of the many different types are shown below.

Dzungaripterus
(wingspan 13 ft)

Dimorphodon
(wingspan 4 ft)

ARCHAEOPTERYX

(Ar-kee-op-ter-icks) "ANCIENT WING"

Those aren't dinosaurs, but ancient birds. They aren't very good at flying!

They use their long clawed fingers to climb up trees, (*right*) and then open their wings to glide down from the top, catching insects on the way. Unlike modern birds, they have small teeth.

It took Sam several minutes to gain control of the machine. Finally, she managed to slam on the brakes, and they screeched to a halt. They had crash landed at the edge of a lake. But what period was this? It was clearly still the land of the dinosaurs, though a bit cooler, and just in front of them Baryonyx was fishing for supper. Then Jools spotted Triceratops in the forest and realized they must have landed in the Cretaceous period. Lucy and Eddie were stranded 80 million years behind them!

These plants look different from Jurassic ones.

What is that?

CRETACEOUS PLANTS
135-165 MILLION YEARS AGO

Bull rushes

Flowering plant

Tree ferns

Swamp cypress

By the Cretaceous period, the effect of herds of dinosaurs trampling and eating the forests has helped the first flowering plants to appear.

BARYONYX

(Bar-ee-o-niks) "HEAVY CLAW"

- **Length:** 27 feet • **Weight:** 2 tons
- **Food:** It catches fish, using its hooklike claw *(above)* like a bear.
- **Features:** Its jaw is like a crocodile's, and behind a row of unusually large front teeth it has lots of small, almost pencil-shaped teeth.

S am tried to start the engines to the time machine but it was no good – water had gotten into the system. Night was falling fast, so they decided to take refuge in a nearby tree.

As dusk fell, the screeches and roars of the daytime gave way to eerie rustlings from the forest floor. Suddenly, two ratlike creatures ran straight up the tree trunk toward them. Jools let out a scream, but Sam quickly shut him up: "Look, they're escaping from that mean-looking creature," she whispered. "Let's hope it hasn't spotted us."

TROODON

(True-don) "WOUNDING TOOTH"

• **Length:** 6.5 feet • **Food:** mammals, lizards, baby dinosaurs • **Features:** It has a large, birdlike head, with huge forward-facing eyes, which means it can see well and hunt easily at night.

It is more intelligent than most dinosaurs, has sharp teeth, and can run very fast, so keep quiet Jools!

First thing the next morning, Sam got to work. The repairs were going to take awhile, so Jools went for a stroll. He wasn't really in the mood for more adventure, but when he heard a loud crash up ahead, he couldn't resist a peek. Three small dinosaurs were attacking a much larger, spiked one.

There was a loud "thud," and a horrible high-pitched screech as the spiked dinosaur caught one of its attackers right on the head with its heavy club. The wounded dinosaur sank to the ground.

Those claws look dangerous!

What is that armored creature?

EUOPLOCEPHALUS
(Yu-op-low-keff-al-us) "WELL-PLATED HEAD"

Bony lids to protect eyes

Club tail

Euoplocephalus has lots of armored features (see diagrams) to protect it. But its belly has no armor, so when attacked it crouches down on the ground.

Bony plates on skin

DEINONYCHUS
(Dyne-on-ik-us) "TERRIBLE CLAW"

Even though Deinonychus is only the same height and weight as a man, it is a fearsome meat-eater.

It has powerful jaws, saw-edged teeth, and a huge claw on each of its twelve toes that swivels viciously to cut into flesh (*right*).

It is also quite intelligent and hunts in packs. This enables it to overcome prey much larger than itself.

Then, with a terrible roar, Tyrannosaurus rex rushed out of the trees! It headed straight for the dazed Deinonychus, and gobbled it up in seconds. The other two ran off as fast as they could, and so did Jools! He raced to the time machine – and T. rex came thundering after him.

Sam had her portable stereo on full blast, and had no idea what was going on. But just then, the engine started with a sputter. With T. rex at his heels, Jools jumped in and flicked the controls...

Let's get out of here!

Help! Look at the size of those teeth!

TYRANNOSAURUS REX (OR T. REX)
(Tie-ran-oh-saw-rus) "KING TYRANT LIZARD"

T. rex

Allosaurus

Coelophysis

At 6.5 tons, T. rex is the largest meat-eater ever. That huge jaw lets it attack plant-eaters twice its size. Its huge teeth are constantly replaced as they fall out.

THE LONE HUNTER

T. rex hunts alone as it doesn't want to share its food. It can run fast, but not for long periods, so it often waits in ambush for its prey. It picks on easy targets, like the stunned Deinonychus, to save energy.

20

Mighty T. rex opened its jaws, and bit into thin air. Millions of years away, the time machine swept Sam and Jools back to the where they had left the others. Eddie and Lucy were anxiously waiting. "Are you okay?" asked Sam. "We got a bit hungry waiting around for you, so we went to look for food," said Lucy. "Just over that hill we came to the seashore and Eddie decided to try his luck at fishing. You should have seen his face when a giant monster leapt out of the water and snatched the fish from his line!"

CREATING SEAS

220 million years ago (or "m.y.a.")

160 m.y.a.
100 m.y.a.

In the Triassic period, the Earth had one continent (*Pangaea*) surrounded by a huge ocean. In the Jurassic period, the seas are spreading as the continents separate.

When Lucy heard Jools' story about T. rex, she was determined to go and see it. Jools and Sam did not like that idea, but as usual, Lucy got her own way! There was no sign of T. rex when they arrived back in the Cretaceous period, so they headed up a hill for a better view.

They reached the top and came face-to-face with a huge hissing head. Sam and Jools froze in their tracks. Eddie even started back toward the time machine! But Lucy had spotted a nest and realized that it was just a mother protecting her young.

Why is she so angry with us?

OVIRAPTOR

(Ove-ih-rap-tor) "Egg Thief"

The maiasaura is afraid that you'll steal her eggs, Sam. The Oviraptor (*above*), is called "egg thief," because of its long fingers and curved jaw. It actually lays eggs of its own and probably sits on them to hatch them.

Nevertheless, it is very likely that some small dinosaurs live off the eggs of larger animals like the maiasaura.

While they made friends with the baby Maiasauras, the Time trekkers heard a deep bellowing noise coming from over the hill.

Lucy, who wanted to see T. rex, rushed over. A herd of Hadrosaurs was moving slowly across the vast plain below.

They had strange crests on their heads, and it seemed as if they were calling to each other. The Time trekkers watched for awhile, but everyone was exhausted by the hot, sticky weather. Lucy, however, insisted they make one last stop, to find out what had happened to all these dinosaurs.

HADROSAURS

(Had-row-soars) "BIG LIZARDS"

Lambeosaurus

Corytho-saurus

Saurolophus: its fleshy pouch shut...

and inflated

Hadrosaurs had strangely-shaped heads. The Saurolophus' nose could even be puffed up like a giant balloon (above)!

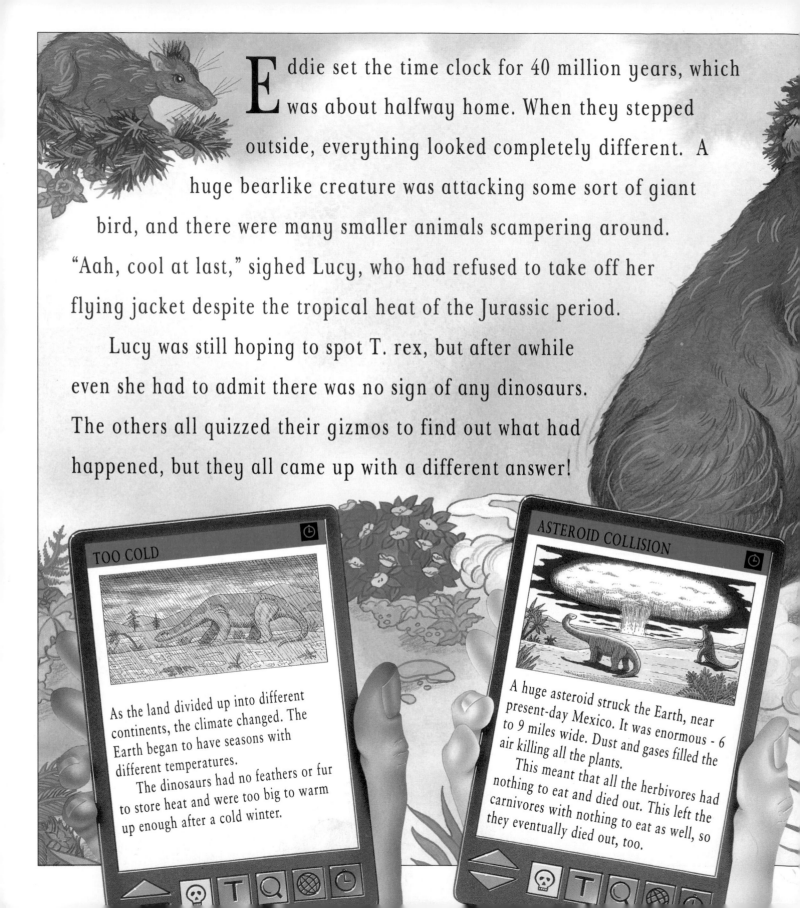

E ddie set the time clock for 40 million years, which was about halfway home. When they stepped outside, everything looked completely different. A huge bearlike creature was attacking some sort of giant bird, and there were many smaller animals scampering around. "Aah, cool at last," sighed Lucy, who had refused to take off her flying jacket despite the tropical heat of the Jurassic period.

Lucy was still hoping to spot T. rex, but after awhile even she had to admit there was no sign of any dinosaurs. The others all quizzed their gizmos to find out what had happened, but they all came up with a different answer!

TOO COLD

As the land divided up into different continents, the climate changed. The Earth began to have seasons with different temperatures.

The dinosaurs had no feathers or fur to store heat and were too big to warm up enough after a cold winter.

ASTEROID COLLISION

A huge asteroid struck the Earth, near present-day Mexico. It was enormous - 6 to 9 miles wide. Dust and gases filled the air killing all the plants.

This meant that all the herbivores had nothing to eat and died out. This left the carnivores with nothing to eat as well, so they eventually died out, too.

The last song on Sam's tape had ended and she had already played it through three times. "That's it, time for home," she said and took control of the time machine. She pressed the button marked PRESENT, and within seconds they were back in her mom's yard.

The other three were all still arguing about what really happened to the dinosaurs. Eddie worked out that they had ruled the Earth for 165 million years.

"That's seventy times as long as humans," gasped Lucy. "And there is nothing left like them... or is there?"

THE GIZMO PUZZLER – SEE HOW WELL YOU DO!

1. When Lucy thought about all she had learned about the dinosaurs and other creatures they had seen, she realized that several had birdlike features. Which were they?

2. Eddie pointed out quite a few similarities to other animals too. Can you guess what they were?

3. Then Jools counted up all the creatures they had seen that were still around.

4. Can you find Jools's frog, Kevin?

THE ANSWERS — JUST TURN THE BOOK UPSIDE DOWN AND LOOK AT IT IN A MIRROR!

1. Triceratops (4) had a beak like a parrot. Compsognathus (6) had a skeleton similar to a model crow. Diplodocus (8) swallows stones that function like a bird's gizzard. Archaeopteryx (13) was an ancient bird, though it had teeth. Pterosaurs (15) are flying relatives of the dinosaurs. Troodon (17) had a large birdlike head with forward-facing eyes, Maiasaura and Oviraptor (23) laid bird-like eggs that hatched their young. Hadrosaurus (25) had long, colourful crests like some birds.

2. Diplodocus (9) had feet like an elephant. Baryonyx (11) had a jaw like a crocodile and caught fish like a bear. Ichthyosaurus (21) was like a dolphin. Plesiosaurus (23) could be the Loch Ness monster?

3. Insects, a snail (6), fish: Baryonyx caught one (21) and so did Eddie (23). Small mammals (17). In the Ancient marine turtles (23).

4. Looking at the Triceratops skull (4), Diplodocus head (7), Falling out of Jools' pocket (13), in the tree (17), On top of the time machine (30).

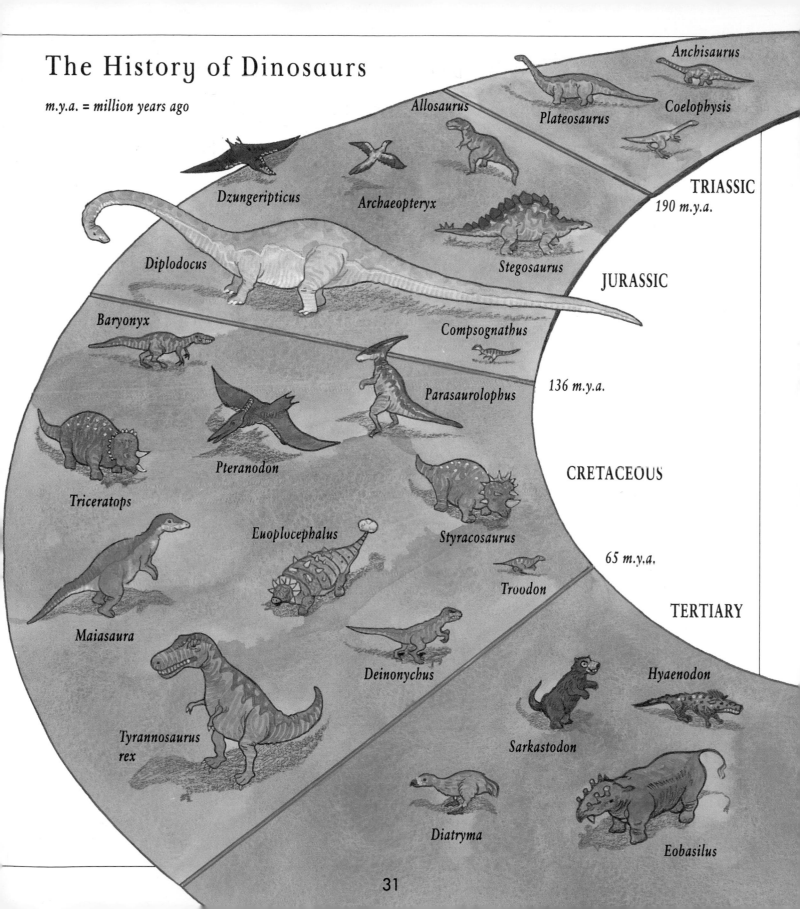

The History of Dinosaurs

m.y.a. = million years ago

Anchisaurus

Allosaurus

Plateosaurus

Coelophysis

TRIASSIC
190 m.y.a.

Dzungeripticus

Archaeopteryx

Stegosaurus

Diplodocus

JURASSIC

Baryonyx

Compsognathus

136 m.y.a.

Parasaurolophus

Pteranodon

Triceratops

CRETACEOUS

Styracosaurus

Euoplocephalus

65 m.y.a.

Troodon

Maiasaura

TERTIARY

Deinonychus

Hyaenodon

Tyrannosaurus
rex

Sarkastodon

Diatryma

Eobasilus

INDEX

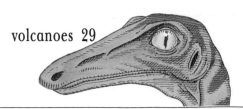